For
Mom and Dad
Happy 60th Anniversary!
Your love for each other inspires me every day
—K—

KAREN SANDAU

grew up in Los Angeles, California she realized early on in life that she loved the wedding business, and she also wanted to become an entrepreneur. In 1999 she became the founder of WedSafe Wedding Insurance and Private Event Insurance. Karen saw the importance of giving the bride and groom a way to protect the financial investment in their wedding from circumstances that are out of their control. Karen is currently pursuing other entrepreneurial adventures in the wedding business.

Karen Sandau

PROTECTING YOUR INVESTMENT

WEDDING
INSURANCE Handbook

TATE PUBLISHING
AND ENTERPRISES, LLC

WEDDING
INSURANCE Handbook

Published by Tate Publishing & Enterprises, LLC
127 E. Trade Center Terrace | Mustang, Oklahoma 73064 USA
1.888.361.9473 | www.tatepublishing.com

Tate Publishing is committed to excellence in the publishing industry. The company reflects the philosophy established by the founders, based on Psalm 68:11,
"The Lord gave the word and great was the company of those who published it."

Book design copyright © 2013 by Tate Publishing, LLC. All rights reserved.
Cover design by Junriel Boquecosa
Interior design by Mary Jean Archival

Published in the United States of America

ISBN: 978-1-62854-819-8
1. Event / Wedding
2. Business & Economics / Insurance / General
13.10.22

CONTENTS

photo by Focus Photography, Inc

FOREWORD

A wedding should be the happiest day of a couple's life, the start to their future. A lot goes in to planning the wedding, from time and stress to a great deal of money. While one hopes that the day will go as smoothly as possible, with very few minor hiccups, sometimes circumstances beyond anyone's control can disrupt the happy day. That's why wedding insurance is such a great investment for brides and grooms to make. Couples can easily recoup losses, from weather disasters to vendor no-shows. Considering the price is minor compared to the overall cost of a wedding these days, it's a sound investment that couples should research and consider. With weather patterns being so severe and unpredictable these days, it's a very good idea for couples to invest a few hundred dollars in wedding insurance to protect their weddings in case the unimaginable happens. Beyond a natural disaster happening on the day, there's the consideration of rebuilding—some vendors or wedding venues may not have the ability to rebuild or if they do rebuild it may not be in time. Having a wedding insurance policy gives couples peace of mind and allows them to recover nonrefundable deposits. Wedding insurance also gives you peace of mind, so you can enjoy the wedding planning process and relieve some of the stress, knowing that you are covered no matter what may come.

—Carley Roney, co-founder of The Knot

Karen's Journey

Karen Sandau had an *ah- ha!* moment in February of 1999 while having a conversation over brunch with Bob Taylor, cofounder of Robertson Taylor International Insurance Brokerage, and his lovely wife, Sue. Karen was expressing her concern about planning her destination wedding in Maui, Hawaii, and that it made her nervous to send thousands of dollars in non-refundable deposits to vendors that she had only met over the phone.

Bob (who is an Englishman) said, "Why don't you insure your wedding?" As it turns out, Karen learned that it is common practice in the UK for the bride and groom to obtain a wedding insurance policy to protect their investment. She thought that it was a great idea and had not been aware that you could actually purchase an insurance policy to protect your wedding. Karen searched for a wedding insurance company online and was unable to find such coverage for her wedding, so she had to forgo a wedding insurance policy for her own nuptials.

Little did Karen know that this brunch was going to be the beginning of a new company that would give brides just like her the ability to purchase wedding insurance online and protect the financial investments in their own weddings.

photo by Focus Photography, Inc

INTRODUCTION

Congratulations, you're engaged! This may be your first wedding or your third wedding, but finding true love is a gift from the heavens above. From here forward, the two of you will be taking on the world together as partners in life. So make every day count, never take each other for granted, trust and respect one another, and you will have your happily ever after.

Now it's time to start planning! You might be having a very formal affair or a destination wedding on the beach; either way, your wedding will be as unique as the two of you are. As you enter the world of planning a wedding, there are times that you will feel excited, nervous, filled with love and joy, and overwhelmed! You will be making hundreds of decisions and spending thousands of dollars.

Surround yourself with loving, positive family and friends who you can count on—they will make your wedding planning process so much easier. A wedding is one of the happiest days of your life and one of the most expensive. That is why I strongly suggest that you spend a few hundred dollars and purchase wedding insurance to protect the financial investment in your wedding. Wedding insurance will also allow you to enjoy your wedding planning process without wondering *what if*. People often ask me, "Why do I need wedding insurance?" There are a hundred answers I can give to that question, but the most obvious is how can you not insure the most precious day of your life? As you stand looking at the love of your life waiting at the end of the aisle just for you, beaming from ear to ear with butterflies in your stomach, overwhelmed with emotion, it will be worth all the hours of hard work and planning!

We decided on a reception venue in my hometown that had great memories for me and my family. We met with the catering manager and put a deposit down to reserve the date. Just a few weeks later, we found out that the reception venue was filing for bankruptcy and closing their doors, taking our nonrefundable deposit with them!

—Tina, South Carolina

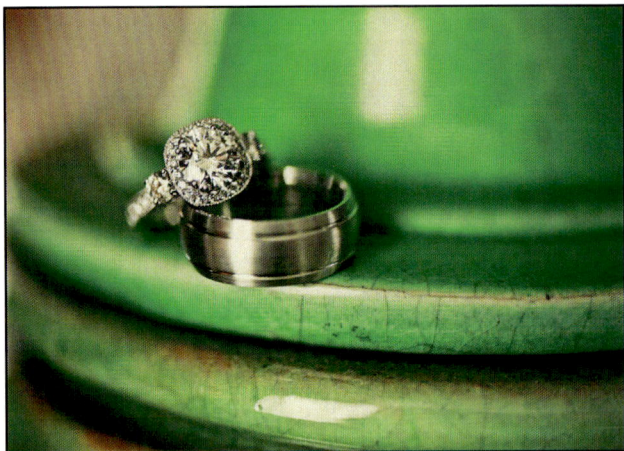

photo by Focus Photography, Inc

Wedding
Insurance

Wedding insurance is designed to protect your financial investment in your wedding from unforeseen mishaps and situations that are out of your control. It will protect you and your wedding throughout the wedding planning process up to the conclusion of your wedding, including your honeymoon. A wedding insurance policy will protect many different components of your wedding such as cancellation, postponement, inclement weather, nonrefundable deposits, sudden illness or injury, no-show vendors, wedding attire, lost or stolen gifts, and much more. Not all wedding insurance companies are the same, so it is very important to do your research and call and ask questions. They cover many more components to a wedding than I have mentioned. Deciding on a wedding insurance company is a personal choice, and you should find one that is right for you and the type of wedding you will be having. Also, make sure to ask questions if you don't understand the policy wording. Call a customer service representative and ask them to explain anything that you do not understand. They should be happy to answer any questions you might have.

Buying a policy will allow you to enjoy the wedding planning process, knowing that you are protected in the event that an unforeseen mishap occurs. You want to make sure that all of your out-of-pocket expenses are covered, especially your nonrefundable deposits. Insurance allows you to relax and enjoy your wedding planning process instead of wondering *what if.* As the founder and president of a wedding insurance company, I can say I have pretty much seen it all, from the smallest mishaps to the biggest catastrophes. I have seen bridal shops go out of business, a father of the bride have a fatal heart attack a month before his daughter's wedding, a groom have an accident on his motorcycle and hospitalized for six weeks and

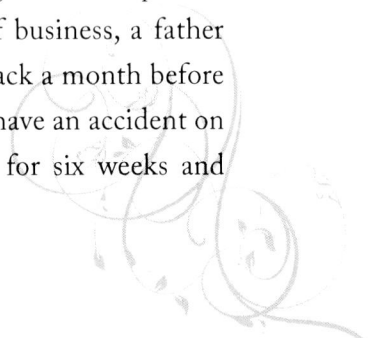

the wedding is four weeks away, a bride twisting and breaking her ankle two weeks before the wedding, and severe weather forcing the bride and groom to postpone their wedding or have to completely cancel their wedding. The examples that I have given are very real, serious, and heartbreaking. I also realize that while planning your wedding, you don't want to think that something may go wrong or a catastrophe might happen, but at the end of the day, we are all human and life happens to everyone.

Our wedding was beautiful, and we had the time of our lives. We thought everything had gone off without a hitch until it came time to gather all the wedding gifts, and we realized they were gone! Wrapped gifts cards, checks, and gift certificates from our friends and family were stolen. Thankfully, our wedding insurance policy covered what we lost; and even though some things are irreplaceable, the memories from that night will be with us forever.

—Sarah, California

photo by Focus Photography, Inc

PURCHASING
WEDDING INSURANCE

The best time to buy an insurance policy is when you put down your first nonrefundable deposit. As soon as you secure the date of your wedding, sign a contract and leave a deposit with the wedding venue, or hire a wedding planner. You need to have an insurance policy in place because you have just spent at least ten thousand dollars. If you are hiring a wedding planner and they are going to help you find a wedding venue, you should buy an insurance policy as soon as you hire and sign a contract with your planner. All weddings are different, and whether your first deposit is on your gown or on the venue, you have now started to leave large nonrefundable deposits with vendors. All of these deposits that you are leaving with vendors are nonrefundable deposits; this is why it is so important that you purchase insurance right away. Buying your insurance policy will give you peace of mind as you leave nonrefundable deposits with all of your vendors.

Wedding insurance is designed to help couples prepare for the financial consequences resulting from unexpected situations such as extreme weather, no-show vendors, and alcohol-related accidents. When things go wrong, it can be frightening how quickly costs can add up. Insurance will cover the nonrefundable deposit due to bankrupt or no-show vendors and the replacement of lost or damaged photographs, jewelry, gifts, or invitations. Coverage also includes the rehearsal dinner, ceremony, reception, send-off brunch, honeymoon, and much more. Every insurance company is unique, so make sure when purchasing your policy that you are getting the coverage that you need. Wedding insurance companies may let you buy insurance as far as two years before your wedding date and as close as fifteen days before your wedding date. Insurance companies have different rules and regulations

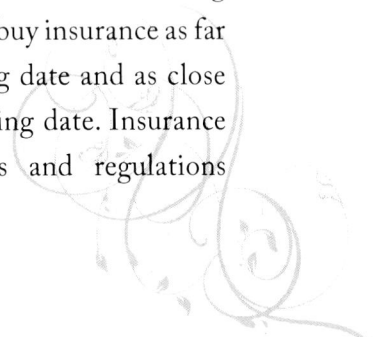

regarding the timing of your insurance purchase, so call and ask the insurance company what their rules and regulations are. Insurance can be purchased over the internet, over the phone, or, in some cases, you may be able to go into the insurance company and purchase the policy in person.

There are a few things that you should look for when choosing a wedding insurance company. You should look for an A-rated insurance company, you can find the rating of an insurance company by going to the A.M. Best website. At the A.M. Best website, you will be able to find out if the wedding insurance company that you are interested in buying a policy from is an A-rated insurance company and not a self-proclaimed A-rated insurance company. You should also look for a wedding insurance company that is in good standing with the Better Business Bureau.

When choosing an insurance company, you should:

- research companies on the A.M. Best website, which will give you the best information for insurance companies
- look for companies with an A rating

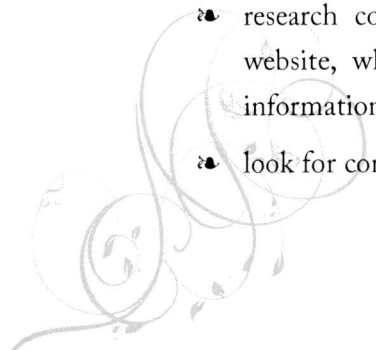

ᴥ look for companies are in good standing with the Better Business Bureau (BBB)

When shopping for a wedding insurance company, do your research online. It is also a good idea to give them a call and see what their customer service is like over the phone. If the company answers the phone and they are friendly, helpful, and are happy to answer your questions, this is a good indication that they will handle you the same way should you need to make a claim or run into an issue with a vendor.

It is very important—and I cannot stress enough—that you must save every receipt and every contract that you sign during your planning process. In the event that you have a problem, postponement, or cancellation, you need to be prepared with the proper documentation to make a claim. Your receipts and your signed contracts are your proof of loss; you will need to provide to the receipts and signed contracts to your insurance company. If you do not have your receipt and your signed contracts, it will be next to impossible to prove exactly how much money has been lost.

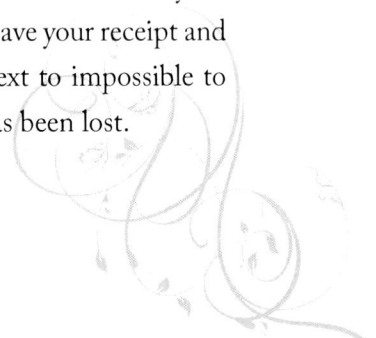

From the onset of planning your wedding, I suggest that you save all of your receipts and signed contracts in a folder or scan them into your computer so that they can easily be found in one place. If you are going to make a claim, postpone, or cancel your wedding, you also must be prepared for the wedding insurance company to ask you for certain documentation. This documentation may consist of letters from a doctor if there has been a medical accident, pictures of damaged goods, and possibly a signed affidavit from the bride and groom. When making a claim with the insurance company, it is standard procedure for the company to do their due diligence to authenticate the claim, and you should not take it personally.

photo by Focus Photography, Inc

WHO BUYS
THE WEDDING
INSURANCE POLICY?

I suggest that the bride and groom buy the wedding insurance policy; however, if the parents of the bride will be paying for the entire wedding, they may want to be the ones to purchase the policy. Regardless, the bride and groom are automatically covered. Whoever purchases the policy will be considered the "named insured."

Modern-day weddings are typically funded by the pooling of money from various family members. The bride and groom may pay for a part of the wedding; the parents of the bride may pay for the majority of the wedding. It is not uncommon for the parents of the bride and groom to split the bill for the wedding as well as the rehearsal dinner. In the event that there is a claim, the wedding insurance company will make the check out to the named insured. It is the responsibility of the named insured to reimburse any money to the various family members that have contributed to the wedding. The wedding insurance company will not make out checks to various family members that may have contributed financially to the wedding. There will be one check made and one check only. It is very important to keep every receipt and signed contract so it can be presented to the wedding insurance company. If you do not have the receipt or the signed contracts, you do not have proof of the purchase, and therefore, you do not have proof of the loss.

Also keep in mind, insurance is usually a very small percentage of the entire wedding budget, so don't be afraid to spend a few hundred dollars that could ultimately save you tens of thousands of dollars in the long run. Make sure that you purchase enough insurance so you are covered for the entire cost of the wedding.

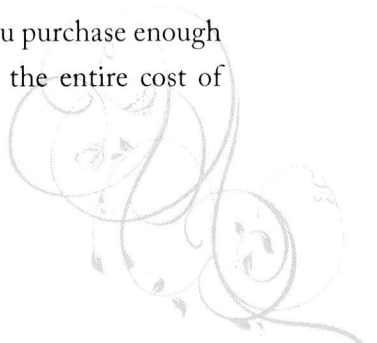

A few months before the wedding, one of my bridesmaids had passed by the bridal salon where I had ordered my wedding gown and saw that the shop was empty! She called me immediately and said that there was a note in the window with the phone number of a law office to call. Needless to say, they did not deliver the wedding gown I had paid for. However, thanks to my wedding insurance policy, I was able to obtain a refund and buy a different gown for my special day.

—Rachel, New York

photo by Focus Photography, Inc

How Much Wedding Insurance Do I Need?

Purchasing insurance is determined by the total budget set for the wedding. You should take into consideration everything that you will be spending money on, and then add about another 10 percent for the items that you did not plan on buying because they will cause you to go over budget. I have yet to see a bride not go over her budget for her wedding.

Once you start shopping for your big day, you will be exposed to so many beautiful items and concepts. Your original ideas may start to change, and may be difficult to say no and stick to a budget.

There are a few other expenses that you may not be aware of that you should add to your total budget.

You should add everything that you are paying for, such as:

- your wedding gown
- bridesmaid's dresses
- tuxedo rentals
- hotel rooms
- airline tickets
- gifts for your bridesmaids and groomsmen
- the honeymoon

You want to make sure that you buy a policy that will cover all of the expenses that you will incur for your wedding in the event that you have to cancel or postpone the day before or the day of. If you have to cancel the day before the wedding or the day of the wedding, you have most likely paid for the entire wedding in full. If your initial budget is $40,000, you need to insure your wedding for at least $45,000 or more as you will likely go over budget.

Be sure to ask your insurance company if they will allow you to increase your wedding insurance

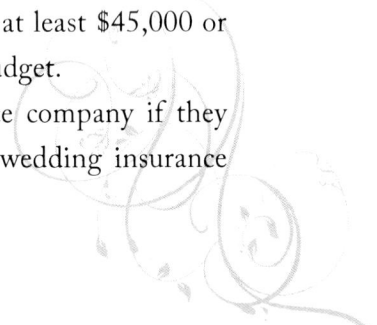

coverage for an additional fee if you go over budget. In the event that you do go over budget, you don't want to have to buy a whole new policy. Also ask the insurance company if Liability and Property Damage is included in your wedding insurance policy or if you need to purchase a separate Liability and Property Damage insurance policy in addition to your wedding insurance policy.

Our wedding was at 3:00 p.m., and the musicians for our ceremony were going to start at 2:30 p.m. as guests arrived. We waited and waited for the musicians, and they never showed up! We had a ceremony without any music, and the musicians had been paid in full.

—Jessica, Hawaii

photo by Focus Photography, Inc

Who Does Wedding Insurance Cover?

A wedding is the biggest production of your life! There will be family and friends who play a key role in this production. Wedding insurance provides coverage for the bride and groom automatically. A policy also extends coverage to family members and friends in the wedding party. Coverage is provided in case an accident or unforeseen mishap strikes one of your key players.

Family members consist of the mother, father, brother, sister, cousin, grandparents, aunts, uncles, stepparents, etc. Friends who are in the wedding party are also included in the policy. The wedding party is usually defined as maid or matron of honor, best man, bridesmaids, groomsmen, flower girls, and ring bearer. Each insurance company will have their own definition of family members and friends, so please read the policy wording, and call your insurance company to clarify who they define as key players in your wedding.

Wedding insurance will also cover you if you lose your job for any other reason except for being fired. You can postpone the wedding, cancel it, or set another date. You will have to provide a letter from your employer, explaining the circumstances of why you were laid off.

We were planning a wedding on the New Jersey Shore at a beautiful restaurant, looking over the boardwalk and ocean. A hurricane hit, and our reception site was demolished. This whole situation was so devastating for the residents of the area that it made our wedding seem like a small issue. You never know what Mother Nature is truly capable of.

—Nathalie, Florida

photo by Focus Photography, Inc

DESTINATION WEDDINGS

Many brides and grooms are choosing to have their weddings at locations all around the world. The good news is that insurance does provide coverage for destination weddings. You may choose a beautiful Mexican beach, a whimsical castle, or a villa in Tuscany. Whatever you choose, the next step is to call an insurance company. You need to ask if they cover the destination of your choice and exactly what they cover and what they don't cover. Most wedding insurance companies cover the United States and US Territories.

If you are getting married out of the country, there is insurance for weddings abroad. A destination wedding is a big deal, and if you are a control freak, you're going to have to give up some of the control as you will not be able to meet some of the vendors and make some of the decisions in person. A good way to gain some control of the wedding is to hire an independent wedding coordinator who is based in the city that you are getting married in. This way, you have someone who understands your vision for your wedding and can convey your wedding theme and style to the local vendors. When getting married in a foreign country, you must do your research on the rules and regulations and what is required to make the marriage legal. The most important factor in planning a destination wedding is the *weather*, so please do yourself a favor and research the local weather patterns. You don't want to be getting married in the islands during a hurricane season!

Three weeks before our wedding, my dad was in a very serious car accident. He broke his back in two places, and we didn't know how long he was going to be in the hospital, let alone the recovery time. Because we had a wedding insurance policy, we were able to postpone the wedding for a year later and recover our deposits. I would never have my wedding without my dad there.

—Amanda, Illinois

photo by Focus Photography, Inc

Military and Armed Forces

Most insurance policies will cover the bride and groom if one or both of them are in the armed forces of any kind. This includes the reserves, coast guard, police department, fire department, and other public service industries.

If you are in the military and are planning a wedding, it is a very good idea to obtain an insurance policy. Most insurance companies will ask for a letter written and signed by your superior officer, granting you the time off for your wedding and honeymoon. This means you must have written permission to take the time off for your wedding and for your honeymoon in the form of a letter signed by your commanding officer. Included in this letter should be the exact dates that you intend on taking leave for your wedding, which will confirm that your commanding officer is fully aware that you are planning a wedding for a particular date, that you intend on being absent for that period of time, and that you have been granted leave.

If you are deployed unexpectedly or your deployment is extended for a longer period and you have an insurance policy already in place, that policy will cover you so that you can reschedule your wedding for a later time. The reason you need written permission by a commanding officer is because this is your proof that you have requested the time off for your wedding, and if you need to postpone your wedding, this will be the proof of loss you can submit to your wedding insurance company to show you did your due diligence.

There are many unexpected things that can happen when you or your fiancé is in the military or armed forces. We never like to think of the worst-case scenario; but when the unimaginable happens, such as injury or death in the line of duty, your insurance policy will be there for you.

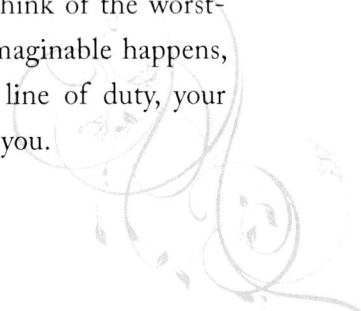

My fiancé and I decided to hire a wedding coordinator who had a great reputation and had a good understanding of the kind of wedding we wanted to have. She had us write checks to her instead of directly to the vendors. We found out that she did not pay any of the vendors, and she took off with all of our nonrefundable deposits along with several other couples'.

—Rebecca, California

photo by Focus Photography, Inc

CLAIMS

First and foremost, if you think you have a claim, do not panic! This is why you have wedding insurance. The next step is to call your insurance company to determine the severity of the potential claim before you arbitrarily postpone or cancel your wedding. You need to confirm with your insurance company representative that you can postpone or cancel your wedding with the problem that you are faced with.

In the event that you do have a claim or need to postpone or cancel your wedding, you will now have to start the claims process. You will be asked a series of questions and will be required by your wedding insurance company to submit your receipts and or signed contracts for your claim to determine the monetary total of your loss. That is why it is so important that you keep every receipt and every signed contract because it is mandatory when submitting any claims.

If you do not have this documentation, your wedding insurance company will not have proof of all of the deposits and transactions that have been paid in full for your wedding.

I strongly urge you to at least purchase a filing system to keep all the necessary documents. Better yet, scan all your paperwork and keep it backed up on your computer and on a flash drive.

Two days before my wedding, I woke up with a temperature of 103 and a sore throat. I panicked and went to the doctor right away. There was no doubt that I had the flu! I had to postpone my wedding; thankfully, because of my wedding insurance policy, I was able to recover all of my nonrefundable deposits.

—Charlotte, Texas

photo by Focus Photography, Inc

LIABILITY
AND PROPERTY
DAMAGE INSURANCE

L iability insurance is an entirely different policy than a wedding insurance policy. A liability insurance policy is specially designed to protect the bride and groom from certain types of claims arising from accidents taking place during the wedding reception and rehearsal dinner. This includes protection for damage to the facility, injury to guests, or alcohol-related accidents that the bride and groom could be found liable for. This is also considered host liquor liability coverage, and since you are inviting family and friends to celebrate with you and you will most likely be having an open bar, it is nice to know that you have coverage in place.

It is next to impossible to manage how many drinks your guests are consuming during your wedding and reception. Some venues require you to obtain Liability and Property Damage Insurance. They may also require you to have the venue added as an additional insured, so it is a good idea to buy it early in the wedding planning process and provide it to the venue as soon as possible. For example, if your guest pushes the videographer into the pool, ruining their video camera, the bride and groom would be able to make a claim to reimburse the videographer for damages up to the insured amount.

TIPS AND QUESTIONS

❧ Decide who should purchase the wedding insurance policy. Usually the bride and groom purchase the policy, but if the parents of the bride are paying for the whole wedding they may want to purchase the policy.

❧ Make sure that you purchase the right amount of coverage to protect your wedding. If you are having a $50,000 wedding, then purchase a wedding insurance policy that will cover a $50,000 loss. Also remember to include the cost of the honeymoon to the total wedding budget, because if you need to postpone or cancel the wedding you will most likely have to postpone or cancel the honeymoon.

- Before you purchase a wedding insurance policy, do your research online and make sure that the wedding insurance company that you choose covers all of your wedding needs. Do not be afraid to call and ask questions. If you do not understand the policy wording, ask a wedding insurance representative to explain it to you.

- When choosing a wedding insurance company, give them a call and talk to a representative and see what the customer service is like. If they are friendly, knowledgeable and answer the phone promptly that is a good indication how they will handle a claim.

- Before you purchase a wedding insurance policy, call and ask a representative how their company handles claims. Ask if they have a representative available by phone after regular business hours, on the weekend, or if they provide a claims department that can be reached twenty-four hours a day.

- In addition to purchasing a wedding insurance policy, consider purchasing a **Liability & Property Damage Policy**, which will protect you

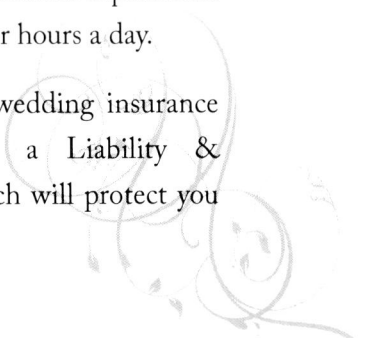

from potential damage to the ceremony site and reception site caused by you or a guest. Ultimately, you will be held responsible for any damage that may happen. It also provides host liquor liability coverage usually in the amount of a million dollars or more.

❧ Some reception sites may require you to purchase a Liability & Property Damage Policy in the amount of one million dollars. The receptions site will also require proof of insurance. I strongly suggest that you provide the proof of insurance at least thirty days in advance of your wedding day. You don't want to realize that you did not provide the proof of insurance to the venue the day of your wedding!

❧ If you are getting married abroad or planning a destination wedding, make sure that your policy covers weddings outside the US. If you are a US citizen and are planning a wedding in another country, this is a good time to find out the rules and regulations that you will be required to fulfill so you and your fiancée can get married in the country of your choice.

❧ Make sure that you check whether your wedding insurance company of choice has an "A" rating with A.M. Best.

❧ Check with the Better Business Bureau to make sure that the wedding insurance company of your choice is in good standing.

CHECKLIST

❏ Keep all of your signed contracts and receipts form all of your vendors you have hired and purchases you have made. You may want to buy a folder to keep them in and organized or maybe scan them and have them on your computer. This is very important because the signed contracts and receipts are your proof of purchases and will be your proof of loss.

❏ You may want to program your wedding insurance company's phone number into your mobile phone so you have it available in the event that you need it. You never know when a question may come up or have a potential claim.

❏ Before choosing a ceremony site, reception site or rehearsal dinner site make sure to ask if they are planning to do construction or renovations of any kind before, on or around your wedding date. If they are you may want to choose another wedding date or different venue.

❑ Remember that wedding insurance is *not* insurance for your vendors. It is insurance for *you*. Most venues insist that the vendor have their own business insurance before they allow them on their property. You may want to ask your vendors if they carry their own insurance.

❑ When booking a ceremony site and reception site, make sure to ask if the property is for sale or in bankruptcy. Leaving a large non-refundable deposit with an establishment that is for sale or in bankruptcy is not a good idea.

❑ If you are planning an outdoor ceremony or reception you must ask the venue if they have the ability to bring the ceremony and or reception indoors if you are faced with inclement weather on your wedding day. Have them show you what the alternative ceremony and reception site is and see if it is to your standards. Also ask them if

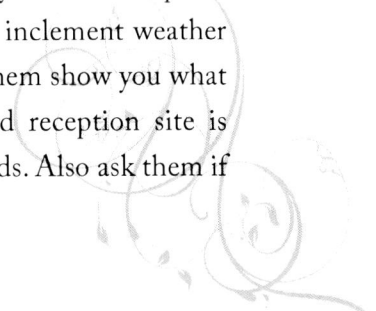

there is an additional charge if you have to move the ceremony or reception inside.

❑ Call all of your vendors at least two weeks in advance of the wedding to make sure your order is correct, and confirm the wedding date and time of arrival for the installation at the venue. Sometimes vendors such as florists take on a few weddings on the same day, so it's best to check with all your vendors.

❑ If the hotel or reception site has assigned a wedding specialist to you, you may want to ask them if they will be your point person the day of the wedding and not an assistant. Also you should ask them if they will be taking their vacation days or maternity leave on or around your wedding date.

❑ One more thing! The planning is over, so let the celebration begin! Leave the stress behind! This is one of the most magical days of your life so enjoy and have fun! Remember your loved ones and friends are all there for you to celebrate this wonderful love you have found in each other.

Whether you have a guest list of fifteen or five hundred, each person has carved out a day dedicated especially to you, so appreciate them and savor every moment!

A Thank You Note...

"At times our own light goes out and it is rekindled by a spark from another person. Each of us has cause to think with deep gratitude of those who have lighted the flame within us."

—Albert Schweitzer

I would like to express my gratitude to the supportive people who have sparked the flame within me, that have contributed to my life and my book.

Carley, thank you for taking the time to write the Foreword for my book. I'm overjoyed!

Janel, thank you for providing your talented photographs for this project.

Steven, thank you for the painting. You are talented beyond words. You are my brother and my friend.

Melody, thank you for your contribution to the book. You are my friend and a very talented woman.

I would like to thank my publisher for believing in my project, Stacy, Trinity, Rachel, Katja, Alexis, Melanie, and Kyle, my editor, who understood me. Thank you to everyone in all of the different departments that had a part in putting this book together from start to finish!

Thank you my loved ones and friends!

R.E.T., Arlene, Scott, Scooter, Steven, John, Cindy, Arthur, Bevin, Amy Pisanelli-McCoy, Sue and Bob Taylor, Angie and the late Willie Robertson, Timothy Mackenzie, MD, Charisse Keck, Evan Liss, and Dr. Sandler.

For all your wedding planning needs go to
www.theknot.com

Focus Photography, Inc.
www.focusphotoinc.com

AM Best
www.ambest.com

Better Business Bureau
www.bbb.org

This *Wedding Insurance Handbook* is presented solely for educational, general informational and entertainment purposes. The author Karen Sandau and publisher are not offering it as legal, accounting, or other professional services advice. While best efforts have been used in preparing this book, the author Karen Sandau and publisher make no representations or warranties of any kind and assume no liabilities of any kind with respect to the accuracy or completeness of the contents and specifically disclaim any implied warranties of merchantability or fitness of use for a particular purpose. Neither the author Karen Sandau nor the publisher shall be held liable or responsible to any person or entity with respect to any loss or incidental or consequential damages caused, or alleged to have been caused, directly or indirectly, by the information or contained herein in the *Wedding Insurance Handbook.* No warranty may be created or extended by sales representatives or written sales materials from insurance carriers or other companies offering wedding insurance policies or related coverage to bind or create liability to the author Karen Sandau. Every individual is different and the advice and strategies contained herein may not be suitable for your particular wedding or event situation. This book is not intended as a substitute for the advice of insurance and wedding coordinator professionals. You should seek the services of a competent licensed insurance professional and wedding planner/coordinator before beginning any wedding or event planning program.

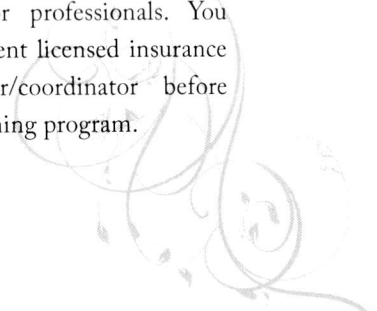